#romance

Jess Green graduated from Liverpool John Moores University with a degree in Creative Writing in 2010. Since then unemployment has forced her down to the Midlands. She is a member of London's Roundhouse Poetry Collective and performs regularly around London, the Midlands and the North West.

#romance

Jess Green

To Katie
I hope you
enjoy the
poetry in this book,
you have cool parents
to be hanging out
in the poetry
tent!

Jess x

holdfire
LIVERPOOL

Published in the United Kingdom in 2012
by **holdfire**.
13 Stormont Road,
Garston,
Merseyside,
L19 1QG

ISBN 978-0-9572724-6-0

Cover Image: *Untitled.* 2008 by Edward Coyle

www.edwardcoyle.co.uk

For the Greens.
For all the money leant,
pints bought
and tantrums listened to.

#romance

Jess Green

Scratch Your Degree

I walk the mile from my house through Toxteth,
the finger prints of one limbed children
washing from my Primark trainers
peeling off my feet into the street litter puddles.
I dig in my rucksack for a pile of rejection letters
and Janet at the job centre
with name badge and ponytail
says, 'love,
scratch your degree from your CV.
It'll make you more employable,
'cause no-one wants a show off,
afraid to get your hands dirty
then off to the theatre.'

So rewind the time back
to before Dad's hatchback
pulled out of the drive
and he imparted the wisdom
not to do acid alone
but to make sure at some point
that I did dabble.

Give back the cap and gown,
take the photos from Grandma's mantel piece,
I never shook hands with Brian May,
and in any case
that would have been ok
because I only know the words to
Don't Stop Me Now
from drinking Baileys in Tom's Mum's kitchen
when she was on her annual caravan holiday
and I was only pretending to like it anyway.

Siphon the Home Bargains fizzy wine
back in to the bottle
step out of the Pilgrim,
Mark's girlfriend would probably thank me
if I wasn't there to encourage him
to drink twelve double whiskeys
just to see what happens,
so let them celebrate themselves in the sun,
have one less night on the feminist pedestal,
no-one will be disappointed.

Drain the coffee down the sink
and freeze dry the beans back into the jar
I always drank too much then sat shaking at my laptop,
scrawling paranoid through ex boyfriends' Facebook pages
while flatmates were out
doing actual drugs,
with real boyfriends.

Take the bottles back to Bargain Booze,
at the time I felt they'd lubricate my stanzas
but they slowed up and preoccupied my rhyme
until I was scratching lengthy verse
about that bitch at work
who probably still at this moment
is thinking up new and inventive ways
to piss me off.

Store away the sonnets
and the useless ancient monologues
leave me with a school born hatred of Shakespeare
lock Prufock, Keats and Browning
in the campus library
on that half of a bottom shelf
in the basement
known as
'the poetry section.'

Take away the words that hurt until they healed,
bury Ariel with Sylvia,
drag the winter dawn down,
unclench my jaw
like he never touched me at all.

Silence the discovered rhythm behind the words
and sooth the itch in my feet and hands
and my sister helpfully inputting
that 'no-one listens when you're waving your arms around,'
but the words can't come fast enough
and I can't do a poem sitting down.

Cling on to that relationship
I only ended for inspiration,
marry him and make his tea.

And when they ask you what you did for three years,
say,
'nothing.'

Another one broken

Out of all the hotel rooms
you left me alone in
it was the one by the coast
where I felt most lonely.
Watching 7pm slide by
like the tides outside
knowing the clock mocked
your promised time,
wouldn't stop for lateness
or pause this knot crawling up inside
or calm the flood of futile anger
that smashed the bright lights of sense
and took with it
the words of self-help friends
who prided themselves on fixing me over a pint.

I don't know how to tell people about you
so generally I make it a rule not to,
but maybe if I put this down,
fix it with syntax
and shout it at a crowd of strangers
like every other common crisis
then it might make it right
and the nerves of feeling could grow again.

That night by the sea
I drank champagne from the bottle
in the blustering wind of an open window,
the mugs were still stained with tea
and you said you'd bring back washing up liquid,
in fact you promised.
Another one broken,
like all the ones about
phone calls
birthday presents
loving me.

You came in unapologetically,
told me off for smoking
so I lit another while you phoned her,
gave her a true tale
of the conference heavy day you've just had
but a fictional prediction
of the evening
you were about to embark on.
'Just telly and bed,'
you tell her.
We didn't even have a telly,
you were too stingy to get a room with one.

I should turn this now,
twist it round
to say it wasn't always like this,
but it was;
I was just too absorbed in you
and being nineteen
and so desperately wanting to be fucked up
so I'd have something to write about,
I couldn't see the vacuum of dissimilar feeling between us.

That night you slipped from a dinner party
to the garden
to phone me and tell me to look at the moon
I was just coming out of Bargain Booze on Hardman Street
and I didn't look
because I hate that sort of crap
but I did stop walking in surprise.

You ended that call
by saying
'baby, I'm so shy and embarrassed around you'
and I wondered what you could possibly want from me
to come out with something
as manipulative as that.

I wasn't allowed to phone you just whenever I wanted,
although sometimes towards the end I did
just to show you I could.
But normally there was an allotted time,
your walk from my old college
to your house on the other side of the park
twice daily.

And that was just a ten minute distance
to get your fix in
so you didn't want to hear about the mundane,
you craved conversation coated in filth.
So the time I tried to tell you
about how Sarah's drug dealer boyfriend
broke in to our house
and put his foot through our TV
you stopped me,
said you had your key in the door
and you had to go.
So you didn't get to hear
about how it took the police
twenty seven minutes
to get there,
because even though he had a kitchen knife,
it wasn't an emergency
until one of us was bleeding.

All those seedy, secret
weekends away
when you so much
wanted to be that Bill Murray character
in Lost in Translation,
to make this arty, sepia, soft tone,
a Plath and Hughes affair.
Let's mess each other up so much
'till we can't feel the guilt
searing through all those
nice good person
ideas we have about ourselves.

I just remember how the room widened
and the silence grew
when I finished my book
so I tried to force sleep
and bored unconsciousness
under covers
but I could see my breath
and there were never enough jumpers,
so I just huddled under cheap hotel sheets
and thought about how
if one of us died,
fell drunk in to the waves,
no-one would think to look here first.

Then travelling home
on the slow Sunday night train,
changing and stuck in the falling frost at Wigan,
turn up my headphones
so I won't have to wonder if that weekend
was even worth it.

You realised too quickly
every time I tried to leave you,
pulled me back
by saying
that I wouldn't have the guts to go
'cause I couldn't do it alone.

But evolution taught us
survival of the fittest
and it was dawning that you were fossilising me,
singeing all my nerves of feeling
like the malnourished Coeliac sufferer
still gorging on toast every morning,
and all the little villis
in their stomach

start shrivelling up
and giving up
and can't absorb any of the good stuff,
too beaten by the temptation
of a daily bacon sandwich.

So I just stopped answering the phone,
faked a heavy hangover head
that couldn't hear your walk to work ring,
began to peel myself off you
until one night
I threw my sim card away
in a red wine haze.

Although I moved on quickly,
met men who seemed to find it
all too easy to say they were falling for me,
I couldn't even feign the same.
Couldn't pump one drop of love
into someone else's veins.

You got in touch last week with a text
asked what I'd been up to
said you'd heard a couple of my poems
and you liked them.

I couldn't reply,
because I just wanted to
ask for my feelings back,
like I want to feel the pain
of when some guy doesn't call
and you don't know
if he likes you anymore
because I've heard that hurts
more than anything.

Beyond the Kettle

Sweaty palm
locked in sweaty palm
at five o'clock on a Thursday in December
when smug suits
said yes please
to two tiered education.

Placards fell in the child revolution,
the son of a rock star dismounted the cenotaph
forgetting why he was even there in the first place,
scuttled back to Eton, apologising.

One colossal society
whittled down to one man
lying through his teeth
releasing the police
to charge on horses
like seventeenth century cavaliers,
beating back children
in the name of civil unrest,
bloody and dazed
surrender caused by bleeding on the brain.

Raise the bar
to the highest degree,
dress it in blue
and then claim it was always like that
we've just been looking the wrong way.

The electorate crowd's been looking down,
scraping pennies off the tarmac,
storing them in jam jars under the bed
because they won't touch the banks.

Ministers dance two step
to avoid recognition,
axing teenage ambition,
laughing at their apprenticeships, BTECs, GCSEs,
competencies and qualities
because if they haven't got the quantity
to get beyond the coach station
prospectus in hand
they're slapped behind the counters of fast food chains,
sat on the spit shined steps of job centres
and benefit offices,
slotted in the slit of a statistic,
published slap bang
front page of the
Daily Hate.
Where's their dignity?
Why so apathetic?

The young ones,
the under tens
won't miss what they never knew,
ban the mention of Higher Education
except for those rated gifted and talented
because they may prove useful
but even they must keep quiet,
not let on
there's more to life
than fighting time to make ends meet.

Only the initiated will travel on closely guarded trains
from platform nine and three quarters.
Ipads locked in suitcases,
Kindles in jacket pockets.

A year six class take a trip to the North West
to see some ancient history.
Lecture theatres, libraries, students' unions
in broken brick rubble,
a sociology text book,
an encyclopaedia of fine art
blowing away.

Potatoes

I was lonely when she first arrived
in a house so huge
it spent some time in the eighties being flats
then bought by a man who turned it back,
filled it with paintings, chandeliers
and miss matched lampshades
but in a way that wasn't Kitsch.

From an attic room
shaded by the street trees in the summer
I heard feet press floorboards
but rarely got a chance
to match a face to the sound;
a month's worth of evenings
sat chin on knees
amongst packed up boxes,
watching David Tennant Doctor Who
and drinking till I fell asleep.

I was angry at my job in a students' union
that I had hoped would help change my bit of the world
but actually just saw me filling in
endless Excel spread sheets
under the glare of a power mad student president
who had a thing for hockey boys.

The night the new flatmate was due to arrive
I set myself against her
and the private school she worked in,
went to The Grapes
and slagged her off till closing time.

Woke vomit throated
to discover I'd scrawled her a note
offering her free reign over my shampoo
and that she had thanked me
in her neat boarding school handwriting.

We bonded over my lack of potatoes
and her having some fried with blue cheese
and the next night
gnocchi and Parma ham.
I told her I was intimidated
when I took my beans on toast out the microwave,
she laughed and said
'you learn variety in dinners
when your parents abandon you age six
and only reappear when you win a lacrosse match.'

She was amazed that I would stand up
and speak my secrets to strangers,
she said she had to see this,
and unlike everyone else who's ever said that
she actually did;
she came to every gig for a year.
Even the weird ones in Egg Café
where the man in his pants
blacked up and said he was the middle of the butterfly
who had lost his wings.

She always sat in the front row
and always cheered the loudest
even when nobody else did.

We drank the Limoncello
my sister had given me
in the pantry
as I filled her in on seeing our landlord naked
and when she laughed so hard
it came out of her nose
and made me cry
I bent double
gripping the cupboard,
had to run to the toilet
and only just made it in time.

She taught kids who paid for the privilege,
she brought home piles of marking
alongside £100 vouchers to canapé bars
in return for moving Benedict up a set in a maths.
She laughed at their bribes
and we had one of the best nights of our lives.
stumbling on so much champagne
that we both agreed wasn't as tasty as a pint of Strongbow
but fuck it,
it was free.

In the dim light,
stuffing as many puff pastry things in as I could
before anyone got the chance to take them away
we guessed at who the mistress' were,
and those that weren't,
whether they were still having sex
or just going home to lie in beds of notes,
keeping themselves warm and satisfied inside
in the knowledge that their stocks were doing fine.

I went to the toilet six times that night
just to use the waterfall taps
and Dyson dryers,
to pout in the complimentary lights
and floor to ceiling mirrors
and when the voucher was dry
we toddled up to Alma De Cuba
and bought glass buckets of wine,
sat in a candle lit booth
as feather tailed Flamenco dancers
moved around us,
met men with bad shoes
who didn't stand a chance
but we took their cocktails and compliments
and laughed when they didn't see
we were laughing at them.

Then swapped our heels for the trainers in our handbags,
slid into the basement bar of Heebies,
danced to the Motown band
with men we wouldn't have minded taking home,
slipped a pill on the dance floor
with a can of Red Stripe
and thought we were literally the best people in there,
with moves like this
we were great,
we didn't even speak
just punched the air
and hit our heads on other people's sweat on the ceiling
when the beat of Proud Mary kicked in.

Even though she said she hated the stuff
when she was sober
every blind drunk night
we stumbled back from
she pestered me to roll a spliff,
then laughed so hard she couldn't tell me what was funny,
made me dance to Outkast
and when the landlord banged on the ceiling below
we turned it up
because he was a perv who had come on to both of us.

In the always darkness of winter
when it snowed so hard
the buses stopped running
I had no idea how I was going to get home
and I was tearful anyway,
I'd had the shittest day;
I hadn't met targets,
I'd got a bollocking,
my shoes had a hole in,
my feet had got wet when I'd gone to get lunch,
she appeared outside work
in her maroon estate car,
told my boss to fuck off,
she could park where she liked.

When we got home she hanged her speakers
down the middle of the staircase,
played Things Can Only Get Better
by D:Ream on repeat.

She had money and land
and was so privileged
she didn't need to understand politics,
she said she loved Coronation Street
because it was a side of life she'd never seen.

She dropped her marking and everything
when I came in with a face on,
let me get into her bed in the middle of the night
when it had all gone wrong
and another one had left,
she got out the emergency wine
that we drank through a straw
as she soothed my bruised ego
with stories of her Match.com phase.

When I ran for re-election
in the student union
and fat Darren ran a hate campaign against me
with the tag line
'stick up for the brothers'
she was the only one
to stay up all night
traipsing around town
taking their posters down.

And when the cheers went up from the banter boys
on the other side of the bar
at the news he'd beaten me
she squeezed my hand
because we both knew
that meant I wouldn't be able to pay rent
in two months' time.

On the morning that I closed the door
on that empty attic room,
I shut my eyes
and didn't cry
until I was safely down the M6.

Some nights
when I stumble back to my Mum's house,
trip over the cat,
I pour myself another wine,
stick my headphones in
and have a one woman Tina Turner party
she'd be proud of.

#romance

I used to not pay much attention to Twitter
but as news spread
that love was blossoming
just a hundred and forty characters away
and that they were the online ones to watch
for December
I flipped from Facebook tagging
and followed the public flirting
as avidly as the rest of their
seven hundred and fifty four followers combined.

She was a flag waving humanist,
liked the arts, tree hugged, comedy and politics.
He didn't have a bio but links to all three of his blogs
full of pale naked ladies,
definitions of love
and seven and a half word long sentences.

They met over a mutual hatred of Matt Smith;
hashtag 'Baker is best',
an online campaign
which they were proud to be part of
but their Twitterspheres collided
when both realised that everyone else meant Tom
when they meant Colin.

'You too?' he asked
'but of course! Why can they not understand?
He's the unsung hero of the space time continuum
from his first appearance as Commander Maxi
in Arc of Infinity,'
'Nineteen eighty three!'
they simultaneously tweet,
blushing furiously from their separate corners of Middle England.

They swapped a couple of videos;
she suffixed Tuesday afternoon's clip
with a cheeky wink.
Those that have followed him for a while
know that he is a Plato Playboy
and at 9.15am on Wednesday morning
during his ritual hashtag train time tweets
he throws out
'And what Socrates is the food of the soul?'
The rest of us are bleary eyed, just trying to make it through our coffee and
cornflakes
scrolling through headlines
about why the dole queues are getting longer,
but she catches on, throws back
'Oh, Socrates the fool, LOL!'

He has authors following him
and he wants her to notice
but in a roundabout away
so Follow Fridays just four
with the line
'here's some friends you could get to know.'

And she's agog because she's a writer too,
except she's experimental,
spells words with baked beans on her belly button,
hangs a camera from the light fitting,
slows down the shutter speed
and wiggles on the floor.
She twitpic'd the image
and while we squinted, turned our iphone screens this way and that
he replied
'woah, cool snap.'

From then on they berated politicians
with satirical wit;
'don't believe the newspapers,
the MPs

or anything you read
'cause we make up our own news.'
Their profiles screamed these social anthropological observations
sitting in the corners of coffee bars,
thumbs on fire,
invisible under thick fringes,
sipping black teas.

But 'LOVE ME!'
she'd type
then delete
and replace with
'yeah, I think Gok Wan is an oppressor of female liberty too'.

One windy Friday night
on the edge of our seats
as she tweets a link with the line 'maybe see you there ladies?'
and in seconds he replies that he too
will be at the Reclaim The Night march tomorrow at six.

Our online timelines run electric,
we wish they'd use a hashtag so we could keep up with the trend,
not miss a trick,
but they don't realise we're watching,
too wrapped up in cyber courtship.

The trail runs quiet
and we wonder what's gone wrong,
refreshing screens all through X Factor
but silence from both sides,
then she spits
'I am never trusting a man with my heart again, where's the vodka?'
and he capitalises
'YOU ARE CULTURALLY BARREN WITH THE EMPATHY OF A DOORMAT.'

As the night grows cold
it seems that he turned up in a Cyberman t-shirt,
doesn't he know they are the most patriarchal extra-terrestrials yet?

Twitter is lonely now they've unfollowed and blocked each other,
gone their separate ways,
I've started following more Coronation Street stars
in search of scandal
but it's not the same.
Even the whinings of Cheryl Cole,
drunk on the dust and mosquitos flying round her brain,
can't fill the void
of the faceless flag waving humanist
and the three blogged boy.

Midnight soliloquies

For Sham

Gangs set fire to your uncle's house
and as the flames scorch the Nairobi sky
I'm waking up in Toxteth
on an electric blanket,
hearing your half voice
in the swamp of part sleep,
the intonation curling high
on the middle of sentences
then locked tight and growling.

A dripping Monday sky pulls me in to morning
but I search with padlocked eyes
for your words in the swaying hours,
thick and drooping,
hanging smoking from the window
requesting Kenyan rap on Youtube
because your fingers won't work the guitar.
Then your silk unconscious words
on the pillow,
passing out in your clothes,
our respective partners oblivious.

Together we were brilliant.
Together our voices spun and wove
and filled the corners of pubs with reverberating tapestries
as we argued over the no mores.
No more poverty,
no more greed, no more crime,
no more David Cameron, no more Twilight.

Now I meet puff chested men racing beers in bars
with their burp filled banter
and hot air thick with testosterone.
They make a game of grabbing women,
matching cop offs with Sambuca shots,
but they don't want to talk about changing the world.

I go on dates
but they can't argue through the candle light like you,
don't want to debate the Lynx advert,
call me antagonistic
and leave.

When your emails are pocked
with full stops and consonants
I want to hear your words
crack through the North West roads
like the speakers that used to thud in our bones
and pounce around our brains,
'cause now you're dancing in my sleep sodden ears
like the radio tuning out
and I don't know what's made up
and what's you.

I can't even write about you
without drowning you in adverbs
those *ly* words that just decorate the verbs
when all I want to say is what we did
and how I still hear your whispers
and the cluck of your tongue at the end of a Tusker
and the rhythm of your syllables
when you're fired up to fight injustice.

But in daylight reality you are soundless
and when I return home to an empty inbox
you are wordless.

Deep down in the Avenues

On these hideaway Friday nights
we sink gin in a ground floor kitchen
while Polish men smoke weed
in next door's garden
and I break your hunter's stare.

Follow the winding banisters
with tripping fingers
along the spiral lamp lit Berlin wall,
twirling through three stories
of half-hearted yellow glow.
We sway up those spirals,
crack egg shell painted walls.

Blurred headed fire skin
on a bed sheet back drop
under the thick spattered sky light,
the invisible wet
not touched by my temperature
it carries the cold
through the cigarette butt streets
and goose pimples the thighs
of girls with Sambuca blood.

Every pushed purple bruise
laced with pulled heart strings
on snapping point
and the pen that's locking you in.

I've got three floors to fill
with passion noise,
desperate lead to the edge
to seep into the plaster, mortar
and single panes.
To fill the clouds
with punching cries
so the rain falls on rooftops
like a need for sleep.

I've lost my time zone
not even pulling back the clock hands anymore
just soaking the saliva out
in the shallow sea deep bath
at 4am
grabbing your short sighted glances.

Outside the taxis shatter puddle water windows.
When I'm gone I scrawl you out in the backs of those cabs.

I sleep still in the thin light
when in hours briefcases will twine
through winter legs
just a bus ride away.

You are awake on my belly button
listening for signs
of where I've been
and who else has been here,
feeding me Christmas chocolates
in the before dawn.

Stop the poetry

You can spend our pensions on dinner with the Beckhams
sack the police
then ask them to work for free
to trick, lie and arrest teenagers
with shifty eyes
and frustrated minds
make us pay to have babies
and glue back our bones
pick the pockets of sixth formers
penalise the unmarried
and patronise the women.
But I will stand on the tables in cafes
on the grass of parks
give me a soap box
or just a flagstone
on a street corner.
I'll light the fuse of villanelles
look down the barrel of a sonnet
blow Blake in the air
and choke the monarchy in metaphor.
My mother warned me about men like you;
you cheat and lie and charm and slime
your way inside
then rip out the life support.
Distract us with a Royal wedding
'look what your life could have been
if you hadn't lacked a little inspiration.'
You can crumble the foundations
on which we've built our lives
but you won't stop the pens moving.
You can't stop me waking
from dream filled sleep
and collect the stained glass stories
from my leaking brain.

Take away our pens and paper
and I'll just make the words move faster,
louder in the corners of pubs
I'll prance along the bar until they listen
climb the walls of buildings;
because if we keep telling the tales of the war you're raging
on the unrich, the unprivileged, the unmiddleaged
they won't forget.
Slap super injunctions
on clause sixty
tell us to calm down
kettle us, keep us, beat us and berate us
but you won't stop the poetry.